Cruising Through the Years

First book of poems by
Chris Oosterbaan and Joyce Snow

Laugh Lines and Other Wrinkles
ISBN 978-1-938911-27-9

Cruising Through the Years

Chris Oosterbaan

Joyce Snow

Full speed ahead

Poems by
Chris Oosterbaan
and
Joyce Snow

Illustrations by
Brian Carey

C&J Lines
Richland, Michigan

Illustrations by Brian Carey

Photography by Terri Cooper

Cruising Through the Years
ISBN 978-1-5136-1641-4

Design and typesetting
Ann Paulson, Paulson Communications

Printing
Cedar Graphics, Davenport, Iowa

TO
Women, Young, Old and Older

DEDICATED TO
Our daughters
Anna and Molly
Once little girls,
now strong women
who share our love
and sense of humor.

TABLE OF CONTENTS

SENIOR STATUS

THE GOOD OLD DAYS

Life was much easier, considerably breezier
When the phone was attached to the wall—
One didn't have to ponder, "Is it near? Is it yonder?"
To answer an incoming call.

And weren't our days rosier, and so much cozier
When attendants filled up the tank?
It was nicer by far to sit in one's car
Do we really have progress to thank?

And no denying, there were times when flying
Was pleasant. In fact, it was great!
We weren't wanded and patted, unshod and dehatted
We simply walked up to the gate!

We've found that we must accept and adjust
If we want to keep up with the game
But we can't help but mumble and frequently grumble,
"The way times have changed is a shame."

C. O.

GEEZERS.COM

I joined a senior dating site
The men spanned quite a range
Bald, wrinkled, hunched and squat
And, frankly, some were strange

Mark has married seven wives
He's shopping for another
Joe confessed at 65
He still lives with his mother

One very handsome cyber dude
Seemed bright and quite alert
He caught my single eye, until
I saw he wore a skirt

A tall, attractive David
So full of manly charms
But then beneath his muscle shirt
I spotted tattooed arms

I'll check again tomorrow
There's bound to be a winner
But for tonight—no Mr. Right
I'm on my own for dinner

J.S.

JUST SAY NO TO SELFIES

I don't understand the "selfies"
Revealing so much in one shot
    So close they expose
    An over-sized nose
And all of these wrinkles I've got

I wonder just why people take them
It seems they're now all the rage
    But as for me
    No camera will be
So close to my face at this age

J.S.

SUZANNE

There was a gal named Suzanne
She had a wayward husband
Eventually she dumped the chump
And now he is her *was*band

C. O.

YOUTH

I took so much for granted
I wouldn't do that now
"Youth is wasted on the young"
The saying's true—and how

J.S.

DÉJÀ VU

Where oh where have my glasses gone?
Without them I'm practically blind!
    I've searched all around
    Will they ever be found?
Am I also losing my mind?!

My glasses are not on the table
on the desk, or under the bed
    My eyesight's so hazy
    It's driving me crazy
Oops, here they are on my head.

J.S.

ME AND SOCIAL MEDIA

Snapchat, Instagram, Hashtag, Twitter
Perhaps I will stay in tune
And make the social media leap
When the cow jumps over the moon

J.S.

HURRY, SCURRY

Grab the dust rag and the broom!
Tidy every single room!
Make sure the junk gets stowed away!
The cleaning lady comes today!

C.O.

ELECTION REFLECTION

Watching their campaigns I was a grump
Couldn't handle Hillary, couldn't tolerate Trump
The media kept us on high alert,
Dishing and digging and piling up dirt
Dirt that grew into massive peaks
Of tapes and tweets and Wikileaks
Finally, when it came time to choose
I wished somehow they both could lose!

C.O.

PATIENT PATIENTS

Made a trip to my Doctor's office
Sat for two hours or more
No wonder the doctor's waiting room
Is filled with "patience" galore

J.S.

THE ER

Avoid the Emergency Room
A place you really should fear
Of course something's wrong
But you'll be there so long
New symptoms will start to appear!

C.O.

THE PRESCRIPTION INSERT

I just got a new prescription
I'm terrified to take it
I've read all the side effects
I don't see how I'll make it!

C.O.

VENTING

It's important to vent they say
To get stuff off your chest
I realize I internalize
Which apparently isn't the best.

I'm one of the millions who've found
Our organs will rise up and fight us
Hold everything in—and what do you win?
A dubious prize called gastritis.

C.O.

COFFEE GRIND

Now that we've retired
No more stress and fuss
A good hot cup of coffee
Is the daily grind for us!

C.O.

TISSUE ISSUE

There's lint in my dryer
On the clothing and floor
The issue is tissue
To clean up once more

Tucked in a pocket
I must confess
It went undetected
And caused me this mess

I'm mad as can be
I must get a grip
From now on I'm tempted
To let my nose drip

J. S.

AUNT DOTTIE

I used to frown at Aunt Dottie
Her clothes were all soiled and spotty
Was it due to old eyes that she didn't realize
She appeared disheveled and shoddy?

I'm here at a meeting this morning
In a hurry I rushed from my house
Now what a surprise to my wondering eyes...
An enormous stain on my blouse!

C.O.

MY FIRST MASSAGE

My massage was a gift from a friend
The masseuse seemed friendly and able
    I took off my clothes
    Stripped down to my toes
And proceeded to climb on the table

The masseuse neglected to tell me
To tuck myself under the sheet
    When she peeked in to see
    a bare naked me
She screamed and made a retreat

Poor woman was met with this sight
My body was totally uncovered
    A tush plump and bare
    Stuck up in the air
I doubt she has ever recovered

J. S.

THE GREENEST GRASS

They say the grass is greener
When you reach the other side
So I hopped into my car
To take a little ride

I learned the age-old lesson
When one decides to roam
Alas, alack, just head on back
It's green enough at home

J. S.

WHICH WAY?

You come to a crossroads in life
The street on the left is called Vanity
Around the bend the sign says Dead End
So, turn to the right and take Sanity!

C. O.

DETERMINED

There's only one way to avoid old age
And I'm not dying to do it!
Times may get tough, the waves may be rough
But I plan to plunge in and live through it!

C. O.

ARRIVAL

The trip to old age went so quickly
I've arrived and jet lag set in
Surveying a daunting new landscape
I'm wondering where to begin.

Tall mountains tower before me
Too high, too steep to climb
So I'll look for other adventures
As I'm booked for a limited time.

Clouds dance to the music of birds
Such beauty never grows old
The river of life still sparkles
And I am still panning for gold.

C. O.

BUS STOP

As they huddle at the bus stop
I'm driving in my car
Reminding me once again
How fortunate we are

I could take my life for granted
I surely have a plateful
So when I'm driving past them
I remember to be grateful

J. S.

THOUGHTS WHILE LISTENING TO MY MECHANIC

He: Lady, your carburetor's shot.
Me: Who am I to say it's not?
He: Looks like you need new brake pads too…
Me: Just why, I ask, should I trust you?
He: Plus a catalytic converter.
Me: This guy could get away with murder!
He: I'll crunch the numbers and fill your tank.
Me: And I'll be heading to the bank.

C. O.

DIGITAL RACE

Slow and steady wins the race
Even then I can't keep pace
Just when I learn a thing or two
It's been replaced by something new

J. S.

SENIOR DISCOUNT DAY

I grocery shop on Wednesdays
Whether it's rainy or sunny
Because it's Senior Discount Day
And we old folks save some money

The savings are substantial
But I've learned to act aloof
When I claim senior status
They never ask for proof!

J.S.

JUNK MAIL

I run to the mailbox
seeking letters from friends
all that I find are
    ads for depends
    invitations to nursing homes
    bills I've been fearing
    and coupons for objects
    to aid in my hearing

After I grab the mail stuffed within
I head for the trash can
And throw it all in

J. S.

IS IT REALLY NEWS?

When the screen says "Breaking News"
It's news already broken
No need to ponder over it...
The talking heads have spoken
Hour after endless hour
You'll hear the pundits' chorus
However could we get along
Without them thinking for us?
The newsmen are quite sure we're dense
They seem to take for granted
That we can't handle just the facts
Until they have been slanted!

C.O.

SANS LICENSE

70 is the new 60, they say
And that sounds good to me
With my driver's license tucked away
I'm only 63!

C.O.

TOOTHLESS

I want to sell all my gold
I'll be rich beyond belief
Sadly though, despite the dough
I'll be missing several teeth

J. S.

OH WELL...

Had a senior moment
Didn't know the cause
Can't be so distressing
I've forgotten what it was

J. S.

ESCAPEES

It's getting harder than ever
To keep my wits about me!
Those clever little rascals
Have gone on vacation without me!

C. O.

SOME MOTHER!

Mother Goose was always loose
She had a reputation
When after writing nursery rhymes
She required recreation

She couldn't fight the subtle urge
To date a lot of men
And after each new nursery rhyme
She cavorted once again

J. S.

AT THE AIRPORT

For all who turn seventy-five,
Here's important breaking news:
When you arrive at Security,
You don't have to take off your shoes!

C. O.

WORRY WART

I worry about the price of eggs
I worry about dancers with chubby legs
I worry about ostriches in the zoo
And I worry about you

I worry about a Chinese monsoon
I worry about men on the moon
I worry about a boy named Sue
And I worry about you

I worry about Donald J. Trump
I worry that some white boys can't jump
I worry about the old versus new
And I worry about you

I worry that redwoods will be cut down
I worry the circus will have no clown
I worry that I'll not see Peru
And I worry about you

J. S.

THE TALE OF LITTLE TOE

We were prowling in the dark,
There were five of us in all.
The other four weren't injured
When I crashed into a wall.

They've got me in tight wraps,
Completely out of sight.
I've learned a painful lesson:
Don't be afoot at night!

C. O.

A DREAM

Let's travel somewhere
Though not in a car
We'll wander through galaxies
Hitched to a star

Let's start out walking
As though it's a hike
Then attach some bird wings
To our swift tandem bike

We'll jump on a lion
Fly with a goose
Cling to the antlers
Of a runaway moose

Let's sail over oceans
On a breeze wafting strong
Our two hearts delighting
In the strains of a song

Let's float through clouds
Slip under the moon
Past all the planets
In a hot air balloon

Come with me, Sweetie
I invite you to soar
To laugh and look down
On earth's grassy floor

If that can't happen
I'll imagine it so
My dream will sustain me
'til you're ready to go

J. S.

FOOD & WINE

A COOKING SABBATICAL

My herbs have lost their pungency
The yeast has seen its day
Old recipes hold no allure
They've all been stashed away.

I'm done with cooking up a storm
And though it may seem radical
Before I lose my faculties
I'm going on sabbatical!

C. O.

KITCHEN REDO

Lee redid her kitchen
Pulled out all the stops!
Stainless steel appliances,
Granite countertops,
New cabinets and new flooring...
It's all quite perfect looking
Everything is top notch now
(Except Lee's lousy cooking!)

C.O.

DINNER MENU

I offer my husband two choices—
My friends just can't believe it!
When he asks, "What's for dinner tonight?"
I say, "We've got Take It or Leave It."

C. O.

AFTER THE PARTY

I'd had a dinner party
The guests had flown the coop
Cleaning up was my last task
I felt my eyelids droop

Looking at the mess we made
Put me in a mood
What the heck was I to do
With this left-over food!

Here a nibble, there a nibble
I did my very best
I was stuffed—I'd had enough
I threw away the rest.

J. S.

POTLUCK

Invited to a potluck and told to bring a pie
  Happy to take it
  But not going to bake it
With so many out there to buy

J. S.

ANOTHER MOTHER HUBBARD

Old Mother Hubbard
Went to her cupboard
To get her poor doggie a bone
When she looked in, found a bottle of gin
To drink while she was alone

Old Mother Hubbard
Went back to her cupboard
Now steeped in an alcohol fog
The cupboard was bare but she didn't care
To heck with the mangy old dog

J. S.

TEMPTATION

Second helpings are such a temptation
Whenever, wherever I dine
But the hardest thing to resist
Is an open bottle of wine

J. S.

MEMORY ENHANCER

They say red wine aids our memory
And I'm living proof that it's true
Last time one bottle was empty
I remembered next day to buy two

J. S.

COCKTAILS

My life is coffee to cocktails
Sometimes 8 to 5 is a grind
    But I'm happy at last
    With wine in my glass
And then I find I don't mind

J. S.

NEW DIET

In the morning I grab a few carrots
And throw in a celery stalk
Determined to prove
I'm eager to move
I head out the door for a walk

A bowl filled with fruit for my lunch
With one cracker and one slice of cheese
Not quite to my goal
But I've shown self-control
Handling my diet with ease

By five I find that I'm hungry
And I'm feeling very much thinner
So a big glass of wine
Would really be fine
Before I splurge for my dinner

J. S,

FASHION & BEAUTY

THE PERFECT PURSE

Lord, make me a purse I can carry
Not overly large or too small
    Light as a feather
    Made of real leather
Something not found at the mall

Make it sassy and classy and chic
By Fendi or Gucci or such
    Let me find what I seek
    Inside when I peek
Being comforted by its soft touch

Lord, I desperately need this new bag
Call it a satchel or clutch
    It's been such a distraction
    With no satisfaction
Shopping and not finding much

A tote bag to hold all my goodies
Something too rare for the masses
    A personal issue—
    It must hold my tissue
Plus wallet, cosmetics and glasses

Lord, create a Dooney and Bourke
With a strap that stays on my shoulder
    I'm down on my knees
    And begging you please
I need it before I'm much older

J. S.

WEIGH IN

Whenever I'm on a diet
Here's how I start each day
I strip off my clothes and my jewelry
Step up on the scale—and pray.

C. O.

TRADING FACES

I've tried facials and lotions and cold creams
I don't see what difference they made
Am I comfortable in my own skin?
Is there anyone out there to trade?

C. O.

FASHION STATEMENT

My legs are too stubby for slacks
Thighs way too chubby for tights
    If my boobs looked better
    I'd wear a chic sweater
But that is just one of my plights

My arms are too flabby for sleeveless
Short skirts show wrinkly knees
    But when the skirt's long
    The look is all wrong
I'm asking the fashion gods, Please

Help me select a new wardrobe
Give me a clue what to wear
    And some finesse
    When I go to dress
I really would hate to go bare

J. S.

PANTYHOSE

Pantyhose have seen their day
It's time to throw them all away.
Donning them was such a fight
The waist was always far too tight.

You'd put them on, you'd spot a snag
You'd sit and feel them start to bag
One step and suddenly you'd freeze
The crotch was down around your knees.

But now our legs stand proud and bare
Veins and brown spots, we don't care
The days of pantyhose have passed
Our legs are singing, "Free at Last."

C.O.

GYM DANDY

I just joined the gym and to my dismay
Young ladies were baring their flesh
Though I felt cute in my warm up suit
They all wore spandex and mesh

I did my routine—treadmill and weights
and stood on the balancing ball
It was a surprise, to then realize
I truly just hated it all

J. S.

NEVER GRAY

I'll never be gray
And I'll tell you why
When I see those roots
I'm willing to dye

J. S.

CLOSET FAIRY

The closet fairy visited
Her wand so full of spite
She waved it over all my clothes
And now they're too damn tight

J. S.

BAD HAIR DAYS

You claim you have a bad hair day
I've had those days for years
The few listless strands that linger
Can literally bring me to tears

Day after day dull and limp
I've tried every new brand of goop
Each follicle lacquered with hairspray
I still can't discourage the droop

I stand on my head to add volume
And blow dry with hot and cold air
Though my strands may disappoint me
I'm thankful I still have some hair

J. S.

WISE WOMAN

Here is one thing a wise woman knows…
It's pedicure time when you can't reach your toes.

C. O.

AGING ANATOMIES

FACELIFT

Frannie had a facelift
Her skin was such a wreck
Now her face is smooth and taut
But, oh my lord—her neck!

Frannie is so tickled
She thinks she looks fantastic
I won't be the one to say
Her face now looks like plastic

J. S.

OLD, BLIND MEN

She used to make men smile and swoon
Oozing girlish wiles and charms
She wrapped men around her fingers
and they'd fall into her arms

Now they barely notice her
Though she's still a gorgeous chick
It's not her fault men don't respond
They're old and blind and sick

J. S.

A BOOK REPORT

My brain is muddled and I'm befuddled
How did I get to this age?
    When I take a look
    At my life as a book
I've turned over many a page

In the middle of life as Mother and Wife
I thought I was so in command
    With each new chapter
    "Happily ever after"
Did not always go as I planned

As I look around and see troubles abound
For many who've rounded this bend
    I'm thankful indeed
    My book's a fair read
And I wonder just how it will end?

J. S.

FALLEN

I've slipped and fallen and can't get up
I fear no one will know
But as long as I'm down, I'll rest a bit
'Cuz I've really got nowhere to go

J. S.

TALK

People whisper far and near
Are they sharing secrets dear?
Or are their voices loud and clear
And I've become too deaf to hear?

J. S,

MY LIFE: A CURRENT INVENTORY

Social Security
Medicare
Runny nose
Thinning hair
Gimpy legs
Rumpled thighs
Titanium hips
Rheumy eyes
Flabby arms
Creaky back
Painful joints
Memory lack
Swollen knees
Slower pace
Yellow teeth
Wrinkled face
Flattened feet
Deafened ears
What I've earned
Through the years

J. S.

PATCHWORK

Look at this face, what a disgrace
    And the body beneath is a crime
The wrinkles now go
From forehead to toe
    I could easily shoot Father Time

Being this age, isn't a stage
    And here is the craziest catch
I'll just go along
Ignoring what's wrong
    There's too much disaster to patch

J. S.

BROKEN SCALE

Oh dear, my scale is broken
Poor thing just doesn't work
It reached a sky high number
Clearly having gone berserk

J.S.

NEW BOOBS

Elaine just had a boob job
On that her appearance rests
She may be full of wrinkles
But she sure has perky breasts

J.S.

TRUE STORY

The last time I took a bath
I wrinkled up like a prune…
I got in at 9 a.m.
And was stuck there ‘til nearly noon!

C. O.

SLEEPLESS IN KALAMAZOO

Night times are not the sweetest
  I toss and turn with twinges.
Time to ask the orthopedist,
  What happened to my hinges?

C. O.

NEWTON’S LAW

Remember Isaac Newton?
He watched the apple drop
And as it fell, he knew darn well
He couldn’t make it stop.
Hard as I try, I can’t deny
The truth in what he saw
My body can’t fight gravity
No! That’s against his law.

C. O.

SPOTS

When we get to a certain age
Every woman understands…
Those little brown spots on your fingers
Show you've got time on your hands.

C. O.

LOOSELY SPEAKING

A loose woman I'm certainly not
But loose skin I've certainly got
My eyelids are falling
My arms are appalling
My firm epidermis is shot!

C. O.

LINES BY ERNESTINE HIDEAWAY

Many many years ago
I was one hot mama
I wore sleeveless dresses then
Just like Michelle Obama

I don't know how or why or when
I lost my girlish charms
But parts of me you shall not see
Farewell to upper arms

C. O.

THE ME I USED TO BE

With apologies to Joyce Kilmer

I think that I shall never see
Myself the way I used to be
Myself in outfits neatly pressed
Against slim hips and youthful breasts
Myself who ran around all day
Lifting graceful arms to play
Myself who did in summer wear
Scant bathing suit and flowing hair
Upon my bosom one has lain
Such intimacy now causes pain
    Poems are made by fools like me
    Still whining for what used to be.

C. O.

HIP HIP HOORAY

She went through hip replacement
She took the bullet and bit it
Maybe someday she'll be able to say
"I'm so happy I did it!"

It's all about therapy now
Stretching and lunging, Ouch! Ouch!
When she's done, after all that fun
She limps to her hot pad and couch.

C. O.

HIS AND HERS

It has been a steady process
We've noticed through the years
The hair on top of his head
Has found its way to his ears.

As for me, it's plain to see
That just below my mouth
My chin has met some others
And followed them down south!

C. O.

BAGGY EYES

Early to bed, early to rise
And still I see bags under my eyes

C. O.

BRAIN TRUST

When your brainwaves are waving goodbye,
It little behooves you to cry...
Forget all the chatter about your grey matter
You've still got some fish to fry!

C. O.

LIVING IN THE MITTEN

JANUARY

Icicles dangle from freezing eaves
And snow now covers the autumn leaves

FEBRUARY

Our pond's an icy winter bed
The hills cry out for ski and sled

MARCH

Our snowy winter so long desired
Has stayed too long—our wish expired

APRIL & MAY

Earmuffs in April, mittens in May
If this is Spring, we hope it won't stay

JUNE, JULY & AUGUST

At first we loved the warmth and sun
We swam and had some summer fun
The drought then wrecked the garden bed
Weeds all sprouted but flowers are dead

SEPTEMBER & OCTOBER

The greens were fading as leaves turn and curl
A kaleidoscope of color as winds blow and swirl

NOVEMBER

Leaves are still turning, piles left for burning
Wet snow now covers them all
I can't remember a whiter November
What's up with this Michigan fall?

DECEMBER

The trees are all bare, it's 30° below
It won't stop blowing and snowing
There's ice on the lake, in this frigid landscape
Only the potholes are growing

J.S.

Family & Friends

BACK SEAT DRIVER

I've been driving for 60 years
Never had so much as a scrape
    But my husband will speak
    From the passenger seat
Critiquing each move that I make

Sometimes I ignore his advice
And pretend I'm driving alone
    But lately I find
    More peace of mind
When I leave the old codger at home

J. S.

MY OLD FRIEND

Just ran into a great old friend
I hadn't seen in years
Too busy with growing children
And with our careers

Years ago she'd been like family
Godmother to our son
I recalled those celebrations
Where she added so much fun

I wanted to reconnect
She looked so much the same
I vowed to call her soon for lunch
But what the heck's her name?

J. S.

TWINS

Double your pleasure
Double your fun
With two darling babies
Instead of just one

Double the diapers
The bottles and such
Double the smiles
You'll welcome so much

Double the laundry
The feedings at night
Double the pleasure
Of holding them tight

Double the crying
That's no illusion
Double the love
Amid the confusion

With two babies at once
Grandmother wins
Double blessings for all
When a family has twins

J. S.

YOUNG'INS

They talk about their periods
So painful they have to cry
Then come the horrid hot flashes
Have you got 'em?
Neither do I!

J. S.

HASHTAG: BEWARE

Beware, all you techie young mothers:
Your family could hit the skids
If you spend more time searching Google
Than you do looking after your kids!

C. O.

TRUE FRIENDS

Some folks are fair weather friends
Close by when life's fuzzy and warm.
　　But the friends to rely on
　　Have a shoulder to cry on
And umbrellas to share in a storm.

C. O.

THE NEW ENCYCLOPEDIA

It used to be parents were experts
Fielding questions 'til they were weary
But technology trumped them
Now when questions stump them,
They call on that know-it-all, Siri.

Children are no longer latch–key
In fact, they are never alone
Siri's beside them
To answer and guide them
As they grow more attached to their phone.

And what does this say about families?
Can we keep the unit alive?
The future's a blur
Dare we ask her—
Dear Siri, will we survive?

C. O.

WEDDING VOWS

When I spoke my wedding vows
I may have made a blunder
For better or worse I promised
Just how much worse I wonder?

C. O.

OLDER WIFE'S TALE

Girls, don't go believing those fairy tales
The truth is somewhat alarming
Because, my dears, in a matter of years
Just look what becomes of Prince Charming.

He gets a bit paunchy, his humor gets raunchy
He's allergic to buying fresh flowers
He can't seem to hear your voice, loud and clear
He watches TV by the hour.

Birthday bashes and such, he'll say are too much
No more calling you Sweetie or Honey
Don't let it hurt you. He'll be blind to your virtues
But he'll keep a sharp eye on the money.

And when he retires, watch out for those liars
Who call the Golden Years, Heaven
Your Prince, in due course,
   will be thrown from his horse
Then you're stuck with him 24–7.

C. O.

GRANDDAUGHTER

My granddaughter, just turning six
Is the sweetest of all my kin
This morning she said,
As we snuggled in bed,
"There's a hair on your chinny chin chin."

C. O.

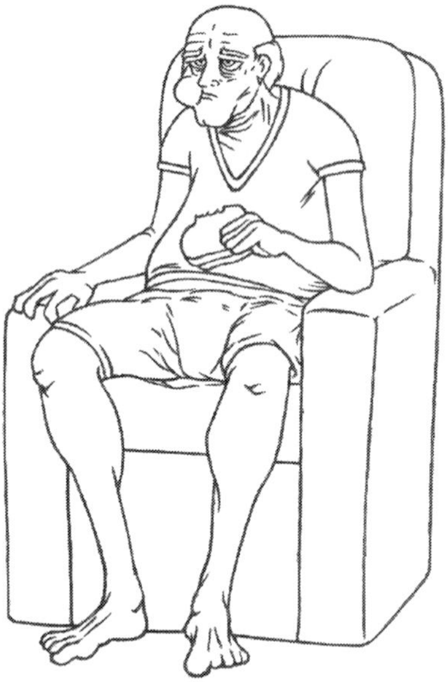

GLORY DAYS

He once was a businessman
A guy at the top of his game
Dressed to the T, sharp as could be
Everyone knew his name.

He relished those two hour lunches
Drinks at his beck and call
While his pert little secretary
Was overseeing it all.

Now he's home with You Know Who
Day, after day, after day
Sitting around in his undies
Munching a P. B. & J.

C. O.

OLD HUBBY

You know him inside-out by now,
His tone of voice, that look
You know what he is thinking...
You can read him like a book!

Be glad he's so predictable,
Like the sun that always rises...
You're no spring chicken, Dearie
Your heart can't take surprises!

C. O.

MY HOUSE

Appraising my house—where to begin?
This is the bathtub my babies splashed in
Here is the cabinet where kids' games are stored
Candyland, Parcheesi, the old Checker board
This is the fireplace that kept us all warm
When the heat went out in a cruel winter storm
This is the window where in darkness I'd wait
For our boys who too often came sneaking in late
These are the stairs our daughter walked down
Smiling and sure in her lace wedding gown

Yes, this is my house, too big for us now
We could pack up and leave but I don't see how
People advise—"It's time. You should sell"—
But this is the house that knows me so well
If these walls could talk, my guess is they'd say
You've been blessed in this house. Why don't you stay?

C. O.

PARADE

My children are marching toward Middle Age
The grandchildren scamper behind
I'm up ahead in the Old Folks' Float
Holding fast to a piece of my mind

C. O.

THUMBTHING TO THINK ABOUT

With the world at their fingertips
They're still not prepared for what comes
So busy texting on their phones
Our kids will soon be all thumbs!

C. O.

GRANDMOTHERHOOD

Oh, you may be enthralled
By a puppy or a kitten,
But a grandchild, oh, a grandchild,
If you get one, you'll be smitten!

Enchanted by the tiny nose,
The precious dimpled chin,
You'll search its face for family traits
(And your family will win.)

You can forget those old-hat roles...
Long–time mother, greying wife
A grandchild makes the whole world new
And you'll be hooked for life!

C. O.

TIME OUT!

When our kids were little, what were we then? Slouches
Just sitting around on our chairs and our couches?
Not driving them 90 miles away
Just to watch a bunch of eight year-olds play,
Not forgetting to sit down as a family to eat,
Not tearing through town to arrive at a meet,
Not letting them go for more practice and training
Two school nights a week when it's cold and it's raining,
Not spending whole weekends focused on sports
Or spending pay checks on jerseys,
    knee pads and shorts,
On ice skates and uniforms and dropping more dough
Just to dress up a kid to look like a pro!

In our day somehow we could not see the reason
For kids to compete in three sports every season.
So, were we slouches, I wonder, complacent and lazy?
Or are parents today on the wrong side of crazy?

C. O.

MOTHER'S DAY

So many lessons we learn in life
Just by living with each other
I was blessed with three children
Who taught me to be a mother.

They taught me that patience prevails
That kids are incredibly smart
That quiet talks in the blanket of night
Uncover what lies in the heart.

They taught me, though it was hard,
To loosen the apron strings,
That they knew the timing better than I
To try out their delicate wings.

They were off on their own in a twinkling.
Still I think of them every day
And theirs are the names that always come first
Whenever I pause to pray.

C. O.

CHRISTMAS IS COMING

LITTLE FAKER

All hail the artificial tree
It's finally okay with me.

Won't have to brave the snow and ice
This little faker will suffice.

Won't have to water anymore
Or sweep up needles from the floor.

So perfectly its lights are strung
Each ornament so nicely hung.

This little tree, so full of cheer
Comes back for Christmas every year.

C. O.

CHRISTMAS CARDS

This year I'm sending Xmas cards
So pretty—green and red
With newsy notes and photographs
So friends don't think I'm dead

J, S,

BAH HUMBUG

Christmas is coming, I am getting fat
And I don't have a penny for the old man's hat

J. S.

WHAT WONDERFUL NEWS

Oh, here it is again, her glowing Christmas letter
And wouldn't you know, as always,
    this year was even better!
She spent two weeks in Paris, learning French cuisine
All those creamy sauces and she still looks fit and lean
Her husband now is CEO, busy as a beaver
He has to travel frequently
    —how can he bear to leave her?
Their daughter was Homecoming Queen,
    their son, star quarterback
They trained their puppy in five days,
    a pure bred lab named Mack
June seventh marked their twentieth
    and just as you might guess
The soirée was "magical." She wore her wedding dress
They bought a Palm Springs condo,
    just a little "getaway"
It overlooks the golf course where famous people play
It's Switzerland for Christmas—they all just love to ski
(A facelift on a chairlift! She looks airbrushed to me!)
She ends with "Happy Holidays!"
    How darling that she said it...
She'll write again next year and,
    once again, I'll dread it!

C. O.

LAST MINUTE SANTA

T'was the day before Christmas,
　　the whole house was hopping
It dawned on him then that he hadn't been shopping!
Off to the mall he flew like a flash,
His credit card maxed and a small wad of cash.
The shops were a blur to his wondering eyes...
What would she want and what was her size?
As he strolled down the aisles,
　　he stopped and he sniffed...
Ho! Ho! It was perfume, his annual gift!
There were so many choices and no time to lose.
All those fancy French names—how could he choose?
He asked the old salesclerk which one he should pick,
Then told her to wrap it up, lively and quick.
The date and cheap price were on the receipt...
He crumpled it up in an act of deceit.
He came home quite merry and threw off his cap,
And went straight to his chair for a long winter's nap
He was just drifting off when we heard him exclaim,
"I need a nap! Wake me up for the game."

C. O.

ABOUT THE POETS

Native Kalamazooans, Joyce and Chris have been close friends since they met as teenagers. Former Soap Box Derby Queens (1956,1957), these two have always found humor in the experiences they've shared through the years.

At college they both majored in English Literature, Joyce at Northwestern University, Chris at Denison University. Joyce was manager of a Hallmark gift store. Chris taught creative writing at the high school and junior high school level.

In 2012 they published **Laugh Lines and Other Wrinkles,** a volume of lighthearted poetry about life and aging. Finding they had more to say, they wrote and published their second book, **Cruising Through the Years.**

Mother of three and grandmother of five, Joyce lives in Richland, MI. with her husband, Don.

Chris and her husband, John, reside in Kalamazoo. They have three children and nine grandchildren.

INDEX

SENIOR STATUS

FOOD & WINE

FASHION & BEAUTY

AGING ANATOMIES

LIVING IN THE MITTEN

FAMILY & FRIENDS

CHRISTMAS IS COMING

Chris and Joyce do readings for groups large or small. For available dates, contact them by

- ❑ Phone: 269-629-9553 (Joyce)
- ❑ Email: C&JLines@gmail.com
- ❑ US mail: C&J Lines
  465 S. Gull Lake Dr.
  Richland, MI 49083

To order additional copies of either **Cruising Through the Years** or **Laugh Lines and Other Wrinkles**, please send check or money order to:

- ❑ C & J Lines
  465 S. Gull Lake Dr.
  Richland, MI 49083
- ❑ Single copies are $14.95.
- ❑ Shipping and handling is $3.00 per book
- ❑ Michigan residents please add 6% sales tax. ($15.85)

For information on quantity orders, contact us by
email: C&Jlines@gmail.com
or phone: 269-629-9553